Dare to Dream

Youth Book

Dare to Dream
Series

Dare to Dream:
Creating a God-Sized Mission Statement for Your Life
978-1-4267-7577-2

Dare to Dream
DVD
978-1-4267-7578-9

Dare to Dream
Leader Guide
978-1-4267-7579-6

Dare to Dream
Youth Book
978-1-4267-7580-2

Dare to Dream
Youth DVD
978-1-4267-7582-6

Dare to Dream
Children's Leader Guide
978-1-4267-7581-9

Dare to Dream
Preview Book
978-1-4267-7583-3

MIKE SLAUGHTER

DARE TO DREAM

CREATING A GOD-SIZED MISSION STATEMENT FOR YOUR LIFE

YOUTH BOOK
BY JENNY YOUNGMAN

Abingdon Press
Nashville

Mike Slaughter

Dare to Dream:
Creating a God-Sized Mission Statement for Your Life

Youth Book by Jenny Youngman

Copyright © 2013 by Abingdon Press
All rights reserved.

This book is printed on acid-free, elemental chlorine-free paper.

Library of Congress Cataloging-in-Publication applied for.

ISBN 978-1-4267-7580-2

Scripture quotations unless noted otherwise are from the Common English Bible. Copyright © 2011 by the Common English Bible. All rights reserved. Used by permission. www.CommonEnglishBible.com.

Scripture quotations marked (NIV) are taken from the Holy Bible, New International Version®, NIV®. Copyright © 1973, 1978, 1984, 2011 by Biblica, Inc.™ Used by permission of Zondervan. All rights reserved worldwide. www.zondervan.com. The "NIV" and "New International Version" are trademarks registered in the United States Patent and Trademark Office by Biblica, Inc.™

Scripture quotations marked NRSV are taken from the New Revised Standard Version of the Bible, copyright 1989, Division of Christian Education of the National Council of the Churches of Christ in the United States of America. Used by permission. All rights reserved.

13 14 15 16 17 18 19 20 21 22—10 9 8 7 6 5 4 3 2 1

MANUFACTURED IN THE UNITED STATES OF AMERICA

CONTENTS

INTRODUCTION

How many times have you been asked what you want to be when you grow up? Seems like from the time we can talk, people begin asking about our dream for our lives. As little kids we think we can be anything, right? Whatever we're into at any given age is usually what we want to be. I'd guess a lot of five-year-olds want to be firefighters, superheroes, or princesses.

As we mature, our dreams change and grow. We start to notice what we're good at and what we enjoy. We start to think about what success really means. As young people, we find that our early fantasies have changed to more realistic dreams.

By the time we have to start making decisions to prepare for our future, we begin to think more practically: what is realistic for my situation? How big a dream can I afford? Do I have the grades for that? Do I have the money for that? Do I have the drive for that? Is that even possible? Our answers to those questions help us glimpse what our lives will look like when we move out of our parents' home and set out on our own life adventure.

As you embark on that adventure, here's what I want you to think about: God didn't create us so we could take a haphazard stroll through life. He created us as unique individuals, with unique gifts and a unique story meant to honor God and bless others. A life with

God isn't about passing time until you get to heaven; it's about living God's dream for your life in the here and now.

So right now, while you're still living at home and dreaming about the future, it's the perfect time to decide what your life might look like. And I don't mean how much money you'll make, what your mansion will look like, or what color your convertible will be. I mean: what do you want your life story to be? What contribution will you make to the world? How will your life honor God and be a blessing to others?

These are some of the questions I'll encourage you to think about as you read this book. I want you to have a passion for God's dream for your life. When you live God's dream, you'll be excited to get out of bed in the morning. When you live God's dream and discover your own unique life mission, you'll get a taste of the abundant life that Jesus promises when we live for him.

This book is intended to help you do three things: wake up the God-dream inside of you, start the process of creating a life mission statement, and commit fully to live that life mission as you discover it—even as a teenager. There is no better time to begin than now. My prayer is that you will refuse just to get by in life and instead will say yes to the great adventure God is stirring up inside of you.

Blessings as you discover your God-sized dream!

TO THE LEADER

As you lead a group through this book, you'll want to be sure that all the group members own a book to read and write in. Each chapter is divided into seven sections that are described below. You as group leader may want to read Mike Slaughter's book *Dare to Dream* as a resource, but it is not required as this book is meant to stand on its own.

WATCH THE VIDEO

Begin each session by showing the video. These videos, featuring Nick Cunningham, introduce the topic and scriptural emphasis.

SHARE IN CONVERSATION

After the video, use these questions as icebreakers to get people talking.

READ AND REFLECT

If you have a group of readers, you may want to ask students to read this section aloud during the session. If you and the group prefer, review the section ahead of time and come to class prepared to discuss it.

Dare to Dream

This section is excerpted from Mike Slaughter's book *Dare to Dream*, emphasizing the biblical teaching for each session. Review the material and the Scripture text with your group and discuss the questions.

Go Deeper

These questions and activities will bring together the video, Scriptures, and readings from the book. They will invite students to begin applying what they have learned to their lives.

Build Your Life Mission Statement

One outcome of this book is to draft a life mission statement. In this section, students will create a mission statement, step by step. Students are encouraged to create the statement in a variety of forms: book, video journal, poster, or some other form that group members choose.

Listen for God

Each chapter concludes with a prayer. You can use this prayer, substitute one of your own, or design a prayer activity that includes the group.

1.

WAKING UP

[Jacob] dreamed and saw a raised staircase, its foundation on earth and its top touching the sky, and God's messengers were ascending and descending on it. Suddenly the LORD was standing on it and saying, "I am the LORD, the God of your father Abraham and the God of Isaac. I will give you and your descendants the land on which you are lying. . . . Every family of the earth will be blessed because of you and your descendants. I am with you now, I will protect you everywhere you go, and I will bring you back to this land. I will not leave you until I have done everything that I have promised you."

When Jacob woke from his sleep, he thought to himself, The LORD is definitely in this place, but I didn't know it. (Genesis 28:12-16)

WATCH THE VIDEO

On the DVD, watch the video segment titled "1. Waking Up." Then reflect on the following questions and make some notes. If you are in a group setting, use the questions to discuss the video.

SHARE IN CONVERSATION

1. What is the craziest dream you have ever had?
2. How many times do you hit the snooze button in the morning?
3. If you could do anything in the world, not thinking about money or schooling or what it takes to get there, what would you do?
4. Have you ever considered that God has a dream for your life? Why or why not?

READ AND REFLECT

I'm going out on a limb here and assuming it might be tough for you to get out of bed in the morning. Unless you are that rare teenager who greets the day with a grin, you hit the snooze button a few times, stumble to the shower, sleep through breakfast, and coast through the morning until around lunchtime, when you finally wake up. I know because I've been there.

Other than infancy, your teenage years are the only season of life when people will actually expect that you'll need a lot of sleep. For now, it's endearing when you make an appearance sometime around noon on Saturdays. The truth is that when we're teenagers, waking up is tough, whether we're excited to face the day or not. It's also true, though, that at some point we have to sit up and seize the day.

So here's what we're going to talk about in this book: are we seizing the day? Are we living life to the fullest, or are we just getting by? You know, sometimes we can be in the "just get by" mode and may not even know it. I'm hoping this book will be a wake-up call—without a snooze button. We're going to discover God's dream and say an excited *Yes!* to all that God has in mind for us.

My Wake Up Call (One of Many!)

I have been a lifelong piano player. I began taking lessons as a small child. Early on, people told me I was a natural, and admittedly I knew I was kind of good and had a pretty good ear. I soon discovered that if I could get someone to play songs for me just one time, I could imitate them and play the songs by ear. My first teacher was impressed that I could pick up the music so quickly. What she didn't know was that as long as she played through it once, I could get it. In sneaky fashion, I figured out how to ask for help in such a way that she would play the song for me. I faked my way through my lessons until around age ten, when I switched teachers. It was a rude awakening.

My new teacher wouldn't play the songs for me. She wanted me to read the music myself. Boy, did my enthusiasm for the piano take a dip! I'd never really had to practice; truthfully, I'd never learned how. My new teacher was not impressed at all. In fact, one time as I tried to play my assigned music, messing up just a few measures in, she stopped me and said to try again. Each time I tried, I let out a big sigh of frustration. Finally, around the sixth or seventh sigh, she closed the piano lid to and told me if I sighed one more time I would not be allowed in her studio again. Yikes!

Some might say she was a little harsh, but it was a wake-up call for me, and it worked. I had a decision to make: I could continue just to get by, wasting my time, her time, and my mom's money, in which case I would lose my spot in her studio; or I could wake up and seize the opportunity to improve and achieve. Today, I am so glad that I woke up and started practicing. God has used my gift for the piano in so many awesome ways.

Surely God . . .

I fully believe that God works in and through us, molding and shaping us to live out his dream for our lives. He helps nurture our natural abilities and gifts, awakens in us new skills and ideas, and gives us concern for things he is concerned about. Jacob in the Bible had a dream in which he saw a ladder from earth to heaven. After his dream Jacob declared that God always had been present, and Jacob didn't even know it.

All of us have sacred spaces in our lives, places where we go to feel especially close to God, to find peace, or to seek clarity. But what if we claimed right now that God is always with us, working in and through us? What if we said, "Surely God is here," then sought to grow and dream and wake up to our God-sized dream? Would that change the scope of our dreaming? Would that help us seize our days instead of just getting by?

If God surely is with us and surely has a plan for us, let's not just get by anymore. Let's run headlong into all that God has for us.

DARE TO DREAM

Mike Slaughter on this week's Scripture, adapted from his book *Dare to Dream*:

As an example of a God-dream, let's look more closely at the story of Jacob in the Old Testament. Jacob eventually became a wealthy, successful businessperson in animal husbandry. In Genesis 28, however, he was on the run. Jacob had just tricked his elderly father, Isaac, into giving him the inheritance that was intended for his older brother, Esau. You can imagine that Esau was unhappy about his brother's deception, so their parents sent Jacob to stay with extended family for his own safety. We read, starting in Genesis 28:10, that Jacob left Beersheba and set out for Haran, about a 750-mile trip. Keep in mind that 750 miles was a very long trip, since they didn't have cars back then. That is a lot of miles on foot.

As the night approached, Jacob stopped somewhere and found a rock to use as a pillow. Sounds comfy, right? Do you ever have restless nights? Well, you should know that God often uses restlessness in our lives to get our attention and create change, especially when we find ourselves in a difficult situation.

In his sleep, Jacob dreamed that he saw a stairway resting on the earth, its top reaching to heaven, with angels ascending and descending on it. In practical terms that dream doesn't make much sense. We know logically that there are no staircases or ladders connecting earth and heaven. But think about your dreams. How many of those at first don't seem to make sense?

In verses 13 and 14, Jacob saw God standing on the staircase, promising Jacob and his descendants the land on which Jacob was dreaming. God also promised that Jacob's offspring would become as numerous as the "dust of the earth" and that God would protect Jacob, never leaving him until the promise was fulfilled. Genesis 28:16-17 describes Jacob's reaction:

> When Jacob woke from his sleep, he thought to himself, The Lord is definitely in this place, but I didn't know it. He was terrified and thought, This sacred place is awesome. It's none other than God's house and the entrance to heaven.

As he did for Jacob, God has created for each of us a unique part to play in his creative plan. God is trying to get our attention, so we can live that plan, and he will not leave us until the plan is fulfilled in our lives. That is what I call "living the dream," and it is what I believe I'm experiencing in my own life. I am living God's dream for me, and I don't want you to miss yours! Life is too short.

Go Deeper

1. Where would you say your life is headed right now?
2. What is your current dream for your life?

Look at Job 33:14: "God speaks in one way, in two ways, but no one perceives it." We often miss God's voice the first time around because of noise, concerns, and routines. But at night he can get our full attention.

> In the dream, a vision of the night,
>   when deep sleep falls upon humans,
>   during their slumber on a bed,
>   then he opens people's ears,
>   scares them with warnings,
>   to turn them from a deed
>   and to smother human pride.
> He keeps one from the pit,
>   a life from perishing by the sword. (Job 33:15-18)

1. How is it possible to miss God's voice?
2. What are some things that might distract us from hearing God?
3. Has God ever spoken to you at night, in a dream?

God also can speak to us through visions when we are awake. Look at Acts 9:10-12:

> In Damascus there was a certain disciple named Ananias. The Lord spoke to him in a vision, "Ananias!" He answered, "Yes, Lord." The Lord instructed him, "Go to Judas' house on Straight Street and ask for a man from Tarsus named Saul. He is praying. In a vision he has seen a man named Ananias enter and put his hands on him to restore his sight."

1. When has God brought someone or something to mind and you knew you needed to take action?
2. Are you a daydreamer? What things do you daydream about? How might God reveal something to you in a daydream?

BUILD YOUR LIFE MISSION STATEMENT

Throughout this book, you will be crafting a life mission statement. As you work on your life mission statement each week, you will have the option of creating a book, poster, or video journal that can serve as an official document for you. Using that document, you'll be able to look back at your dream and gauge how near or far you are from the dream becoming reality. You'll also be able to make adjustments as you grow wiser and closer to God through prayer and Bible study.

This week, your task is to identify three people you admire, and consider the following questions about them. Make good notes here, because the notes will help you create your final statement in the last chapter.

- What are the greatest qualities that you think these people exemplify?

- What steps have these people taken to nurture the qualities?

- Why are the qualities important to you? How would your life be different if you began to live out those qualities?

Listen for God

Gracious and loving God, I realize that my dreams might be too small. Give me eyes to see who you made me to be and courage to walk into the future you have for me. Help me not to be satisfied with going through the motions, but to choose each step carefully. Be a light unto my path. Amen.

2.
WHO IS AT THE TOP
OF YOUR LADDER?

After Jacob got up early in the morning, he took the stone that he had put near his head, set it up as a sacred pillar, and poured oil on the top of it. He named that sacred place Bethel. (Genesis 28:18-19)

WATCH THE VIDEO

On the DVD, watch the video segment titled "2. Who Is at the Top of Your Ladder?" Then reflect on the following questions and make some notes. If you are in a group setting, use the questions to discuss the video.

SHARE IN CONVERSATION

1. What is your favorite movie? Why is it your favorite?
2. What's the best story you've ever heard?
3. Have you ever considered who is at the top of your ladder or at the other side of your vision?

4. Is God the one directing your path, or have you been going it alone?
5. How has someone else been a blessing to you by living out their dreams?
6. How can your dreams be a blessing to others?

READ AND REFLECT

If you took all your Facebook updates, tweets, Instagram photos, and Pinterest boards and laid them out in full view, what kind of story would they tell? I mean, what would you find out about your life? What would someone else find out? Maybe you would see a great life with great friends. Maybe you'd see a love of sports or music or fashion. Maybe you'd see words that bless others and point to a life with God. Maybe you'd see a desire to change the world. Whatever you'd see, I want you to think with me about the story your life is telling, and not just in social media. We tell a story with our lives, and it's up to us to choose whether it's an action-adventure, a messy drama, or an altogether rotten tomato.

Consider with me some options about how to live our lives. We can just muddle through, head down, and get by. We can race through, leaving whatever and whomever in our wake. We can look out only for ourselves, ignoring any concern for others. Or we can look to God, walk with purpose, be a blessing to others, and live with intention. It depends on who or what is our focus. It depends on who or what is at the top of our ladder.

Remember the story of Jacob and his dream of angels going up and down a ladder? Well, God was at the top of that ladder. Jacob saw God at the head of it all and knew that God would fulfill his promises to and through Jacob. Who is at the top of your ladder? If it's God, then you can bet that your life will tell an awesome story and that God will finish the work started in you.

Part of the reason we can get stuck in a small dream or in our comfort zone is that we're afraid. We're afraid of the unknown. We're afraid that we're not good enough, smart enough, whatever enough. . . . We're afraid of trouble. We're afraid of what other people will think. We're afraid of being afraid. Sometimes I've been so afraid of saying yes to God that I've felt completely trapped and unable to take a step forward. But then one time I heard some wise words from Gary Haugen, the president of the International Justice Mission (IJM), an organization that fights human trafficking around the world. Haugen wrote, "Our Maker asks: 'Do you want to be brave, or do you want to be safe?'"[1] Jesus never said, "Come follow me. You'll make lots of money and live in a big house and nothing bad will ever happen to you." He said, "Give everything away. I am all you need, and the God of the universe is on your side." He said, "Go to the ends of the earth. Feed the hungry, clothe the naked, make a difference, and bring heaven to earth."

That's the story I want my life to tell. I want a God-sized vision for my life that packs in significance, meaning, and heaven-on-earth moments. I want my life to be more about blessing others and pointing to God than gathering possessions and patting myself on the back.

What about you? As you dare to dream about a God-sized mission for your life, what is your story? Who is the main character? What's the plot? Would you want to watch the show? I hope you'll take this as a challenge to put God first in your life, make your life about blessing others, and bravely say an emphatic *yes* to God.

DARE TO DREAM

Mike Slaughter on this week's Scripture, adapted from his book *Dare to Dream*:

We talked earlier about Jacob and his dream. In the dream he saw a staircase, or ladder, with angels going up and down. Most important, though, was what Jacob saw at the top of the ladder. It was God. Stop for a moment and ask yourself what's at the top of your ladder. Your life dreams will be limited by the ceiling of your life pictures. What limitations are your life pictures placing on you?

When Jacob saw God at the top of the ladder, God revealed not Jacob's day job but the life mission for which Jacob was created, in the form of God's promise of countless offspring and enduring protection. Let's continue Jacob's story:

> After Jacob got up early in the morning, he took the stone that he had put near his head, set it up as a sacred pillar, and poured oil on the top of it. He named that sacred place Bethel. (Genesis 28:18-19)

At that point, God had really gotten Jacob's attention, and Jacob was beginning to recognize his God-dream. Jacob then made a promise to God:

> "If God is with me and protects me on this trip I'm taking, and gives me bread to eat and clothes to wear, and I return safely to my father's household, then the LORD will be my God. This stone that I've set up as a sacred pillar will be God's house, and of everything you give me I will give a tenth back to you." (vv. 20-22)

I love God's patience. Did you notice all *ifs* and *buts* implied in Jacob's response? The Lord would be his God *if* Jacob was protected, got food to eat and clothes to wear, made it back to his father in one piece, and on and on. There were so many conditions to his commitment! To move forward, Jacob would have to lose his "big buts," which we will talk about shortly. For now, though, Jacob was at least beginning to understand God had a dream for him that was greater than being a successful herder.

In fact, God had a change-the-world purpose before we were born, not just for Jacob's life but for all our lives. You might think, "Who, me?" But the Book of Jeremiah proclaims, "I know the plans I have in mind for you, declares the LORD" (Jeremiah 29:11). And Jesus said, "I assure you that whoever believes in me will do the works that I do. They will do even greater works than these" (John 14:12).

Don't let the scope of your dreams be limited by the ceiling of your life pictures! Many of us initially respond as Moses did when God told him (paraphrase of Exodus 3:7-11): "I hear the cries of my children who are in bondage in Egypt, and I'm going to send you." Moses responded, "Who am I that you would send me? There are far more gifted people. There are better people. There are people who don't struggle in their faith the way I do, Lord. There are people who demonstrate a higher character level than I do, Lord." Sound familiar?

But here's the thing: God doesn't make mistakes. When God created you, he knew his plan for your life. God won't back out of it. God won't quit. Jacob is a perfect example. Jacob's very name, according to Esau in Genesis 27:36, meant what most of us today would call identity theft. He had taken the birthright and blessing of his brother and was on the run, fearing retribution. And yet God had a great dream for Jacob's life.

Go Deeper

1. What gifts do you think God hardwired into you?
2. When have you felt the nudging of the Holy Spirit to act or do something?
3. What is the role of the Holy Spirit in helping us discover God's dream?
4. How are you equipped to serve God and serve the world?
5. When have you felt that when God asked you to do something, he picked the wrong person?
6. What keeps you from believing that God could do an amazing work in and through you?
7. What fears hold you back from saying yes to God?
8. What story do you want your life to tell?
9. How can you begin to tell that story, even now?

Build Your Life Mission Statement

Continue to work on your life mission statement. By now, you should have chosen to create a book, poster, video journal, or other kind of document that will express the statement. This week, your task is to answer three questions that will help you discern how your gifts might meet a need in the world. Make good notes here because they will help you create your life mission statement in the last chapter.

- Where do you see the greatest need around you in your neighborhood, your community, or your world?

- How can you meet that need?

- What gifts do you bring to further that mission?

LISTEN FOR GOD

Gracious and loving God, I am both in awe and terrified that you would choose to use me as a vessel of your love in this world. Remove my fears and plant in me a bravery that causes me to say yes when you call. Show me the vision you have for my life. Let my life tell a great story of who you are and what you're all about. Amen.

3.

DISCOVERING YOUR
BURNING BUSH

There the angel of the Lord *appeared to him in a flame of fire out of a bush; he looked, and the bush was blazing, yet it was not consumed. Then Moses said, "I must turn aside and look at this great sight, and see why the bush is not burned up." (Exodus 3:2-3 NRSV)*

Watch the Video

On the DVD, watch the video segment titled "3. Discovering Your Burning Bush." Then reflect on the following questions and make some notes. If you are in a group setting, use the questions to discuss the video.

Share in Conversation

1. What are some of your biggest pet peeves? What offends you most often?
2. What kinds of unfairness do you witness or experience daily? What is your response?

3. When you look around the world or in your daily life, what are some of the situations that make you angry?
4. What causes have you supported? Why did you choose them?

READ AND REFLECT

I mentioned International Justice Mission (IJM) in the previous chapter and the call from the organization's president to be brave as we follow God's call in the world. Let me tell you a little bit more about their work and how it has been a burning bush for me.

IJM is on the front lines fighting modern-day slavery around the world. I had heard of this nonprofit but had never really understood what they did, and to be honest I found it hard to believe that slavery still existed in the world, much less in our own country. Then I went to a concert of one of my favorite artists, and she spoke in depth about IJM and their work. Not only was slavery still alive and well, at that time there were something like 29 million slaves worldwide. As I write this, the number is around 27 million.

In this type of slavery, young girls are kidnapped and sold to brothels, and entire families are bound to factory owners and made to work all day and night without breaks or food. Imagine your family, even your little brothers or sisters, made to work in fields and factories in abusive conditions and in fear for their lives. When I first heard the stories, I felt a fire begin to burn and an anger that hasn't gone away. I felt a call to take action. The first step for me was to join the IJM Freedom Partner program to support them financially. I filled out a card at the concert and started sending payments.

As I learned more about human trafficking, the fire in me grew. When I look at the four little kids running freely and enthusiastically around my house, I cannot bear the thought of a family like mine slaving away for an abusive factory owner. I have become passionate about the work of fighting slavery, but my time is limited. IJM needs lawyers, detectives, government experts, politicians, and law enforcement officials. I don't have the gifts to join them on the front lines. And yet, a fire burns in me.

So what am I to do? Here's what I know: I am not called to go to law school (because I would never in a million years get into one). I am not called to uproot my family and move to Washington, D.C. to work at IJM headquarters. I am not called to be on the front line right now. Instead, I am called to pray, to give, to support, to promote awareness, to write my legislators, to pray again, and then to pray some more. I pray and believe that God will act. I used to minimize the importance of my prayers, as if I wasn't really doing anything and had nothing to give. But right now, prayer is the most important thing I can give. The Bible says that faith in God can move mountains. So I pray and believe that God will act and make the mountain of modern-day slavery crumble into the sea.

You know, there are so many causes to take up in the world. There are plenty of injustices to go around. There is oppression in plain view. You only have to look around to find a place to join the work that God is doing. And when God appears before you in a burning bush, lighting a fire inside of you, my prayer is that you will say yes and invite God to show you what to do next.

DARE TO DREAM

Mike Slaughter on this week's Scripture, adapted from his book *Dare to Dream*:

You have been created to be a part of God's redemptive mission in the world. You weren't sent to Planet Earth just to eat food and make a living; you were meant to experience and carry out God's dream. Part of identifying that dream is to encounter a burning bush.

Let's look at how it happened for Moses in Exodus 3. By that time, Moses had been living in the land of Midian for forty years, taking care of his father-in-law's flock. One day he was tending the sheep near Horeb, known as the "mountain of God," when he spotted a bush that appeared to be on fire and yet wasn't being burned up. Not surprisingly, that got Moses' attention, so he stopped to check it out.

The Lord spoke to him from within the bush, directing Moses to remove his sandals because he was standing on holy ground. Frightened, Moses hid his face. But God went on: "The cry of the Israelites has now come to me; I have also seen how the Egyptians oppress them. So come, I will send you to Pharaoh to bring my people, the Israelites, out of Egypt" (Exodus 3:9-10 NRSV).

Moses encountered a burning bush, and you will too if you look for it. The ultimate hunger, thirst, and passion that all of us feel is to find the reason we were created. Even though we can't always name that hunger, and we often try to satisfy it with other things, all of us want to know our life purpose. And isn't it interesting that the bush wasn't burned up by the fire? When you encounter your burning bush—a defining event that leads you to your life purpose—it creates a fire in you that will not burn out.

Notice that when Moses saw the burning bush he said, "I must turn aside." It's true for all of us. We must turn away from dull daily routines and lackluster lives—from the "same old, same old" that we have been doing year after year. When we change our priorities and replace what's at the top of our ladder, we find our purpose. We understand then, as Moses did, that no matter where our feet happen to be planted, we are standing on holy ground.

A burning bush moment is when you hear God speak in a personal way so that you can know your purpose. When Moses stood before the burning bush, he saw an angel of the Lord. In Hebrew, the word we translate as *angel* means "messenger." When I look back, I see that God has sent many messengers into my life—people who asked me, even as a young child, if I had ever thought about being a minister. How has God spoken to you over your lifetime, and whom has God used to do so?

Notice that Moses' burning bush experience and the mission it revealed were deeply tied to his life experiences. As a baby, Moses had been a target of genocide. Growing up, he had witnessed beatings and ill treatment of Hebrews. As an adult, he saw firsthand the oppression and injustices that the Egyptians visited upon slaves. All these experiences came together at Moses' burning bush.

As you think about your own burning bush, keep in mind that it may be tied to some of your deepest and most painful life experiences. These difficulties may very well be clues to the places or opportunities where God has called you to act.

Your life mission will always be connected to God's redemptive purpose, not your own self-interest. Moses' life mission grew out of his early experiences, but in the end it was an expression of God's will:

Then the LORD said, "I have observed the misery of my people who are in Egypt; I have heard their cry on account of their taskmasters. Indeed, I know their sufferings, and I have come down to deliver them from the Egyptians. . . . The cry of the Israelites has now come to me; I have also seen how the Egyptians oppress them. So come, I will send you to Pharaoh to bring my people, the Israelites, out of Egypt."
(Exodus 3:7-10 NRSV)

God does not invest in our personal agendas. He has called us to invest in his redemptive plan.

GO DEEPER

1. When have you experienced God stepping into your story?
2. Read Psalm 34. What does it mean that God is "close to the brokenhearted"?
3. Who today are the people "whose spirits are crushed"?
4. How close are we to the broken things in our world?
5. How aware are we of the injustices and the suffering of the people we live with?
6. When you look at the world, what bothers you? What isn't okay? What makes you angry?
7. When have you felt a moment of influence and felt led to act?
8. How is God working in your life to reveal his purpose for you?
9. How can you get to know God's heart? How does seeking it help you identify your life mission?

Build Your Life Mission Statement

Continue to work on your life mission statement. By now, you should have chosen to create a book, poster, video journal, or other document that will help express the statement. This week, your task is to answer three questions that will help you identify past and present struggles that can shape your future. Make good notes here, because these will help you create your life mission statement in the final chapter.

- What struggles in your life have you had to overcome? How have those struggles defined you?

- God can use all things to strengthen his kingdom, and we are called to strengthen it too. How can you share the lessons learned from your struggles?

- How have those lessons helped you in the past, and how might God use them to shape your future?

LISTEN FOR GOD

Gracious and loving God, I want to be passionate about your future for me. Show me a glimpse of how my gifts, skills, passions, and desires might come together to do your kingdom work. Light a fire in me to fight injustice and oppression. Give me eyes to see the world as you do. Amen.

4.

EXCUSES

But Moses said to God, "Who am I to go to Pharaoh and to bring the Israelites out of Egypt?" (Exodus 3:11)

WATCH THE VIDEO

On the DVD, watch the video segment titled "4. Excuses." Then reflect on the following questions and make some notes. If you are in a group setting, use the questions to discuss the video.

SHARE IN CONVERSATION

1. What are you most afraid of?
2. Do you sometimes make excuses to get out of doing something you feel led to do?
3. What are your most common excuses?
4. What is the most ridiculous excuse you have ever given?
5. What keeps you from having confidence that God made you for a purpose? What can you do about it?

Read and Reflect

Do you know anyone who is afraid of heights? Maybe you yourself have this fear. Well, I have it. I have to hug the wall on the second floor of the mall and won't let my kids go near the rail. It makes my stomach turn even now just thinking about it, and I am ten miles from the nearest mall.

I don't know when I got this fear. As a child I used to love riding roller coasters, climbing tall trees, and standing on top of jungle gyms. Somehow as I grew older, every year I got a little more afraid. Unfortunately that fear has spilled out into other parts of my life. If I let myself go there, I'd be afraid of just about anything—car wrecks, kidnapping, natural disaster, and alien invasion, just to name a few. Our fears can prevent us from experiencing joy and freely living the abundant life that Jesus promised his followers. We can become frozen in fear and miss the beauty and adventure of a life with God.

Let me tell you a story about a friend of mine who became frozen in fear. At the time, my husband and I were youth pastors. When we took a youth group from Chicago to New Mexico, we decided to come home through Colorado so the kids could see the Rocky Mountains. Most of them had never been west of Illinois, so we thought they would enjoy it.

We went to Royal Gorge, a place you may have visited if you've ever been to the Rockies. You might know that Royal Gorge is a suspension bridge connecting two peaks. The bridge is about 1,050 feet high and about 1,200 feet across. That translates to about 120 stories high and three football fields across. Somehow, though, the bridge hangs securely without any support lifting it from the bottom. But here's the thing about the bridge: you can't just walk across without noticing how high you are. The boards that you walk on have just enough separation that you can look down and see a tiny river 1,000 feet below. And the side rails are such that you can have a completely unobstructed view on both sides. So you are always aware of the tremendous height as you make your way across.

As we arrived in the parking area, we got out of the vans and discussed our plans. We would all spend some time on the bridge, taking pictures and enjoying the view, then meet up for lunch at a restaurant on the other side. Most of the group took off across the bridge and thought it was great. But after a minute or two, I noticed that one of the kids, a young man named Sam, was not moving. Sam was about a fourth of the way across the bridge and was completely frozen.

That's when I realized that I would have to be brave, or at least pretend to be. My own fear of heights had kicked in, and it was all I could do to step onto the bridge. My game plan was to look up and straight ahead until I got to the other side. But Sam was going to need my help along the way. When I reached him, he had tears in his eyes and was whispering that he couldn't do it. He was too afraid. His gaze was down, looking between the slats of wood at the tiny river below. All he saw was fear, and he could not move.

I knew that in order to get across, Sam would have to be stronger than the fear that was keeping him frozen, and so would I. We would need to take steps, having faith that each subsequent step would get us closer to safety on other side. In order to do that, we had to look up. We had to stay focused on the view before us. We had to trust ourselves, trust each other, and trust God to get us through. We took baby steps and stopped a few times to close our eyes and simply breathe. It took Sam and me about an hour, but finally we made it across. When we reached the other side, our team cheered, and Sam finally relaxed and took in the view of the mountains.

When God calls us to do something we think is beyond our ability or comfort level, we can get stuck. We can freeze in place, staring down on all the reasons why we're not good enough or why it's a bad idea. The only way forward is to lift our eyes, focus our gaze on Christ, and take baby steps forward in faith, trusting that God will equip us as we go.

DARE TO DREAM

Mike Slaughter on this week's Scripture, adapted from his book *Dare to Dream*:

Excuses, excuses—we all have them. "*But* I'm not smart enough." "*But* I'm too young to live that dream." "*But* I don't have the money." "*But* that decision feels way too risky." "*But* I'm just one ordinary person."

Frankly, no dream worth pursuing will come easily. There will be obstacles, and there will be excuses—what I call our "big buts." If we are to fulfill God's dream for our lives, we have to lose our big buts, or at least downsize them.

Let's return to the story of Moses in Exodus 3. Moses had just had a God vision, a burning bush experience. Moses was eighty years old, and God told him to leave the land of Midian and return to Egypt, where Moses would take on the pharaoh and his armies and deliver tens of thousands of people from slavery. (Exodus 12:37 tells us the Israelites numbered at least 600,000, not counting the children.) As you can imagine, Moses came up with a boatload of "buts."

I'm Not Qualified

The first big but is in Exodus 3:11. "But Moses said to God, 'Who am I to go to Pharaoh and to bring the Israelites out of Egypt?'" In other words, "God, I'm not qualified."

Do you ever say that to God? Well, rest assured that if you *do* feel qualified, then your mission is not big enough. To put it another way, if you are only doing things you think you can accomplish, then you haven't discovered your life mission. God wants to challenge you and stretch you. God's true purpose for you probably will feel impossible. If that seems harsh, just remember: God said, "I'll be with you" (Exodus 3:12).

I'm Spiritually Unfit

The second big but is in verse 13: "But Moses said to God, 'If I now come to the Israelites and say to them, "The God of your ancestors has sent me to you," they are going to ask me, "What's this God's name?" What am I supposed to say to them?'" In other words, "But God, I'm spiritually unfit. I'm spiritually ill-prepared. I'm spiritually illiterate."

Many of us look at Moses and think that he had it together—that he had an intimate relationship with God. But he didn't really know who God was. Think about it: for the first forty years of Moses' life, he was exposed to the pantheon of Egyptian gods, and as a prince of Egypt he would have been expected to study them all. Then for the next forty years of his life, Moses was in Midian, where his father-in-law was a priest; the Midianites were also polytheistic. Moses probably believed there were all kinds of gods, many of which he had studied and even worshiped. In essence he was asking God, "Which one are you? What am I supposed to tell the people when they ask me your name?"

Here is how God answered Moses' second big but: "I Am Who I Am" (v. 14). What kind of answer was that? It didn't really address Moses' question. However, it was what Moses needed to hear, because in essence God was saying, "Don't put me in a box." He was reminding Moses, as all of us need to be reminded, that an infinite God cannot be grasped by our finite minds. God is telling Moses, "I am too big to understand, but guess what? I am here with you. I am not uninvolved or impersonal. I see the injustices. I hear the prayers of my people. I am here to do something about it, and I am going to do it through you."

No One Will Believe Me

The third big but is found in Exodus 4:1. (By the way, notice the chapter number. Can you believe that when God put an amazing call on Moses' life, Moses spent two whole chapters arguing with God about it? He was never going to win that argument!) Moses asked God, "But what if they don't believe me or pay attention to me? They might say to me, 'The Lord didn't appear to you!'" In other words, "But God, what if I can't convince them? These people know who I am. I lack credibility."

Moses had a past reputation to worry about. Remember, he fled Egypt after murdering an Egyptian citizen. Moses believed if he went back, he would have all the credibility of a murderer. Moses, like all of us, doubted what God could accomplish through him. We base those expectations on our own understanding of our limitations and failures, and also on other people's opinions.

I'm Afraid

The fourth big but is in Exodus 4:10. Moses told God, "My LORD, I've never been able to speak well, not yesterday, not the day before, and certainly not now since you've been talking to your servant. I have a slow mouth and a thick tongue." In other words, "I stumble over my words. I'm afraid to speak in front of people."

Moses appeared to be totally inept and inadequate for the mission God had called him to. So why did God choose him? And why does God choose you or me? Look at God's response to Moses in Exodus 4:11: "Who gives people the ability to speak? Who's responsible for making them unable to speak or hard of hearing, sighted or blind? Isn't it I, the LORD?" In other words, God's power is shown through our inadequacies.

GO DEEPER

1. When have you been paralyzed by fear? How did you get through it?
2. Review Moses' excuses for why God shouldn't use him. How did his excuses reveal his fears?
3. What fears keep you from saying yes to God? How do your fears turn into excuses?
4. How aware do you feel that you are of God's presence in your life?
5. What steps can you take to put more and increasing trust in God?
6. When have you had to rely on God's strength when your own ran out?
7. Why does God call us to more than we can handle?
8. How can we overcome our fears to follow God's dream for our lives?

Build Your Life Mission Statement

Continue to work on your life mission statement. By now, you should have chosen to create a book, poster, video journal, or other document that will help express your life mission statement. This week, your task is to answer three questions that will help you consider your fears and negative thoughts about your ability to carry out a God-sized mission. Make good notes here, because they will help you create your life mission statement in the last chapter.

• The biggest fears I have about saying yes to God are:

• The negative thoughts that keep me from believing God has something for me are:

•When I feel negativity or fears creeping in, I will:

LISTEN FOR GOD

Gracious and loving God, I confess that I have ignored your calling in my life at times because I am scared. I'm not fully convinced that there is anything about me that you can use. Forgive me for my unbelief and for my chronic excuse-making. Help me to believe that you will finish the work you start in me. Amen.

5.
WHAT'S IN YOUR HAND?

The LORD said to him, "What's that in your hand?"
Moses replied, "A shepherd's rod." (Exodus 4:2)

WATCH THE VIDEO

On the DVD, watch the video segment titled "5. What's in Your Hand?" Then reflect on the following questions and make some notes. If you are in a group setting, use the questions to discuss the video.

SHARE IN CONVERSATION

1. What are people always telling you that you're good at?
2. What are some of your favorite things to do?
3. When have you felt exhilaration because you were doing something that mattered?
4. What is unique about you?
5. Why do you think God made you the way he did?

READ AND REFLECT

Sometimes we overthink things; I know I do. We think we need this or that before something else can happen. We think we need the right kind of weather to get in the right mood. We think we need the right people, the right skills, the right degrees, the right . . . whatever. But you know what? God is all we need. Everything we need in order to accomplish God's dream for our lives, we already have. God made us and has equipped us for the work we are called to do. Everything in our lives—our abilities, our experiences, our hurts, our joys, our hopes—God brings them all together to equip us for our work.

If you haven't already, sometime soon you may be working on college applications. Some applications are daunting, to say the least. Once you get past all the fill-in-the-blank questions, the personal information, and the request for financial aid, you're left with some open-ended questions and statements to write about, such as: "What is the greatest global crisis, and what solutions can you offer?" or "In 2,500 words, describe your greatest dream for your life."

If you're anything like me, this would be the point at which you'd set down your papers, walk away from your computer, and wait for inspiration. You'd convince yourself that you needed the perfect amount of sunshine to be in the right mood to have the perfect cup of coffee at that perfectly quaint little coffee shop. You'd bring out every stall tactic known to humankind, because you have a hard time knowing how to begin essays like these. It seems that you have nothing good to say, no solutions to offer, nothing to contribute.

But the thing about the college essay is that admission counselors really just want to know about the applicant. They want to know the story behind the personal information and the financial need. The crazy questions are meant to help you bring together all your education, experience, and gifts to really think about what you are meant to do. And you are the only one who can fill that blank screen with your story. Sadly, there is no perfect time or place where clarity will break through. You just have to sit down and do it.

The good news is that everything you need to tell that story is in your head and heart. Even if you're not the best writer or grammarian, you have everything you need in order to tell someone who you are and what you're about. You're the one who knows the trials you've faced, the despair you've suffered, the joy you've celebrated, the hard work you've endured, the skills you've learned, the talents you've nurtured.

As with that college essay, all these things are in your hands as you imagine what your God-sized mission might be. Think about everything that has made you who you are today, and let God take it all and blow your mind with what he can do through you.

DARE TO DREAM

Mike Slaughter on this week's Scripture, adapted from his book *Dare to Dream*:

Let's return to Exodus 4, where we examined Moses' burning bush experience. Moses was eighty years old when he learned his mission through the burning bush; thank God he discovered it before he died! Moses ran through his litany of "big buts," but God wasn't about to let him off the hook.

Then, in Exodus 4:2, God asked Moses the critical question: "What's that in your hand?" Moses answered, "A shepherd's rod"— basically a staff, a stick. You know that Moses had to be thinking, "What am I going to do with a stick?" After asking the question, the Lord gave a command: "Throw it down on the ground" (v. 3). So Moses threw it on the ground. It became a snake! What did Moses do? He "jumped back from it"; in other words, he ran or at least thought of running. Looking at our own lives, how often do we run from the work that God is trying to accomplish through us? But God wasn't through with Moses yet:

Then the LORD said to Moses, "Reach out and grab the snake by the tail." So Moses reached out and grabbed it, and it turned back into a rod in his hand. "Do this so that they will believe that the LORD, the God of their ancestors, Abraham's God, Isaac's God, and Jacob's God has in fact appeared to you." (vv. 4-5)

Now, the problem is that you and I tend to focus on what we don't have versus what we do have. Please hear me: in God, everything that you need you have already been given. In God, all the resources required to accomplish the mission you were created for you already possess. God uses our ordinary gifts, talents, and life experiences, which you and I often take for granted, to fulfill his dream for us.

What was the shepherd's staff? It was an ordinary tool that Moses used every day. The terrain where he tended sheep was hazardous and hilly, and at times he used the staff to brace himself and keep from slipping off the mountainside. The staff also served as a weapon if there was an attack by robbers or predators such as hyenas. The crook or curved end of the staff was used to guide the sheep, which I imagine at times could be almost as difficult to herd as cats. The shepherd would slip the crook around a sheep's neck, and since there were no sharp edges it didn't hurt the animal. As soon as the sheep felt the crook, it would be startled and would stop. Then the shepherd could gently move the sheep wherever he wanted it to go. There was no way Moses could conceive how that simple shepherd's staff would be used to fulfill God's mission. It would ultimately intimidate a pharaoh, part a sea, lead people through a wilderness, and bring water from a rock.

Like Moses, we often are oblivious to the simple tools we can use to fulfill God's purposes. As I write this, I'm thinking about my computer keyboard, which I use daily to write and answer email. It's an amazing tool when you think about it, though I don't completely understand how it works. I don't even have to think about where the letters are; my fingers automatically go there. (My little finger is especially familiar with the delete key, because I have to use it a lot.)

It's amazing how God uses our simple tools and the collective weight of all our life experiences, even failures, to fulfill our life purpose. Think about it: Moses became a shepherd through failure. It was quite a fall to go from prince to pasture. Shepherds were on the lowest rung of society, but God used that failure for his redemptive purpose. And it wasn't only Moses' shepherding experience that would come in handy; it was all his life experience. Acts 7:22 tells us, "Moses learned everything Egyptian wisdom had to offer, and he was a man of powerful words and deeds." Notice that it doesn't say he had learned all the Scriptures. So why was he useful to God? Moses knew how to infiltrate the Egyptian culture. He was a student of his contemporary culture and had mastered it.

We are born for and wired for a God-purpose in the world. God's question to you is: "What's in your hand?" Everything you need has already been given to you. Then, as with Moses and his staff, God commands you to throw it on the ground. Once you recognize what's in your hand, you then have to release it to increase it. You have to take what you have been given by God and release it into God's hand. Then you don't take it back again until God tells you to. When God does put it back in your hand, it's no longer just a stick; it's God's stick.

Go Deeper

1. Why do we tend to focus on what we don't have rather than what we do have? How can we change?
2. What do you already have that God can use?
3. What situations have you been through that have shaped you into the person you are today? How is that experience a tool that God can use?
4. How do you think someone else would describe your gifts or abilities?
5. What makes your heart beat fast?
6. How do your passions, abilities, gifts, and experiences come together and point you in a direction toward God's dream for your life?
7. Think about Moses holding that staff in his hand, watching God transform it right before his eyes. Remember that the staff was his primary tool for shepherding. What is your primary tool right now? How can God transform it to use for his purposes?

BUILD YOUR LIFE MISSION STATEMENT

You have one week to go before you put together your final statement. Continue to work on your life mission statement now. This week, your task is to answer three questions that will help you consider how God has placed in you everything you need to carry out his mission. Make good notes here because they will help you create your final statement in the last chapter.

• What are the gifts of my head?

• What are the gifts of my hands?

• What is the passion of my heart?

LISTEN FOR GOD

Gracious and loving God, you are amazing. It's hard to believe the way you take what I have and work through me. But I do believe your promise to live in and through me. Everything I have is yours, Lord. Use me. Amen.

6.
GET GOING

I have let you see it with your eyes, but you will not cross over into it."
And Moses the servant of the Lord *died there in Moab, as the*
Lord *had said. (Deuteronomy 34:4b-5 NIV)*

Watch the Video

On the DVD, watch the video segment titled "6. Get Going." Then reflect on the following questions and make some notes. If you are in a group setting, use the questions to discuss the video.

Share in Conversation

1. What do you think you'll be doing when you retire?
2. Would you be satisfied sitting around a doughnut shop having the same conversation with the same people every day?
3. In five years, what do you want to look back on and see about your life right now?
4. What do you need to do to start living a God-sized dream?

READ AND REFLECT

At the beginning of this book, I told you that this time in your life is the perfect time to discern and dream about your mission in life. These are the days when you're discovering what you're good at and what you love to do. You have the whole world set before you; think of it as a great adventure as you dream about what God has for you to do. But in all your dreaming, remember that even the best-laid plans might take a different shape or form than what we originally thought. Making your life mission statement gives you clarity of purpose, but it doesn't guarantee that you will always know what's ahead or what you should do. Sometimes you just have to step out and let God bring clarity along the way.

For my whole life I've studied music. Everyone always told me that as a grown-up I would be doing something in music. Music has always given me joy and has been my passion, so I believed what they said. Surely I would have a career in music. I sang in every choir I could sign up for. I played in the symphonic band, the marching band, and the jazz band. I took piano lessons and competed regularly. I took voice lessons in college. Music was my life, so naturally I thought it would be my career.

I went to college on a music scholarship and played in bands, sang in choirs, and took private lessons. I declared a major in music education early on, so my classes were heavily skewed to music courses as well. I was eating, living, and breathing music, gearing up for the life that everyone had always told me I was made for.

Well, at the end of the first semester of my junior year I was completely burned out. My grades started slipping, I started to zone out during my classes, I found other things to do besides spend those hours in the practice rooms. I wasn't so sure I was made to be a musician or music teacher after all.

At the same time that my music fatigue was beginning, I was finding a tremendous amount of energy in some ministry and theology classes I'd been taking. I signed up to serve on a campus ministry team and became part of an active college-age ministry. Before I really even thought about it (or talked to my mom, an oversight that I absolutely do not recommend!), I had gone to the academic dean's office to change my major from music to youth ministry. I was probably about ten hours away from a music degree, and I had just added another semester's worth of work to my college career. But I was so burned out that I needed a drastic change. Instead of taking my final round of music classes, I started a youth ministry internship and found myself actually enjoying New Testament Greek. I had no idea what I was going to do after school, but ministry felt like the right path at that time.

By the time I graduated, God had revealed a little more of the plan: I would be headed to seminary. Then, during my three years at seminary, my path shifted again. I began my studies with a practical program that would help me become a professional youth worker or children's minister, but I experienced the same kind of distraction and cloudiness I had felt before. I remember waking up in my little Chicago apartment and praying all night. The next morning, I went to the dean's office and changed from the church-focused degree to a general degree in theology, one that would send me on a search for my theology and my passion for God, and one that would hone in me a love of words and writing. After that, I never looked back. My classes were tailored to my gifts, my papers were a joy to write, and my master's thesis was daunting but never overwhelming. I had no idea what I would do when I graduated, but by that point I knew that God would show up and reveal the next thing to me, and he did.

God sent me to Nashville, where I spent more than ten years in Christian publishing, using every bit of my education and experience. But of course Nashville, besides being a publishing center, is also known as Music City. Music is everywhere, and just about everyone you meet is pursuing or is closely related to someone pursuing music in some way. In a wonderful and unexpected turn, God brought together my training in music, my passion for ministry, and my love of writing, and I exercise all of them nearly every day. What's more, my life mission—encouraging and nurturing families to grow in love with Jesus, and fighting in every way I can against human trafficking and modern-day slavery—is also my day job. I get to write books and songs and speak to people about these things.

I couldn't have imagined what God would do with my training and experiences. But I do know that God will never hide from me. God doesn't create us for a purpose and then keep us guessing forever. God doesn't trick us or string us along. God uses every bit of who we are for God's great work in the world. Every class, every experience, every pain, every joy, every wrong turn, every shattered dream—God uses all of it to equip us to live his dream.

My prayer for you is that, as you begin this dreaming process, you will say yes to God. You may not know fully what that means, but your *yes* sets your feet on a path where he will lead you. As you look into your future and begin to dream and make decisions, know that even if you have to change course, God will be there to light your way. Remember, God led the Israelites with a cloud by day and a pillar of fire by night, and God will lead you to a God-sized mission for your life!

Dare to Dream

Mike Slaughter on this week's Scripture, adapted from his book *Dare to Dream*:

We can see that Moses' God-dream was not going to be a walk in the park. But *quit* was not in his vocabulary. What about yours? What will become of your God-dream when obstacles appear? And trust me, they will. Even at 120 years old, Moses was still receiving a big vision from God. Many of the people I know who are age sixty and up are looking backward and doing less. Yet at the time of his death, Moses continued to have a forward focus. Take a look at Deuteronomy 34:4-7 (NIV):

Then the LORD said to him, "This is the land I promised on oath to Abraham, Isaac and Jacob when I said, 'I will give it to your descendants.' I have let you see it with your eyes, but you will not cross over into it." And Moses the servant of the Lord died there in Moab, as the Lord had said. He buried him in Moab, in the valley opposite Beth Peor, but to this day no one knows where his grave is. Moses was a hundred and twenty years old when he died, yet his eyes were not weak nor his strength gone.

What separates those who *do* from those who *don't?* We find the key in that final verse. When the Bible refers to Moses' eyes, it doesn't mean his physical eyes; it means his focus and ultimate priority. Moses was successful in his God-dream because he had a sustaining vision. This is what Jesus meant when he talked about making blind eyes see: bringing vision to the lost, giving them and us the clarity to focus on the "one thing," the God-priority. Keeping this in mind helps to provide context as we read what Jesus had to say in Matthew 6:22-24 during his Sermon on the Mount:

"The eye is the lamp of the body. Therefore, if your eye is healthy, your whole body will be full of light. But if your eye is bad, your whole body will be full of darkness. If then the light in you is darkness, how terrible that darkness will be! No one can serve two masters. Either you will hate the one and love the other, or you will be loyal to the one and have contempt for the other."

Your eyesight—your vision—has to have a clear focus, without distraction, on the one thing, the God-thing. Many of us are too easily distracted; then the picture gets fuzzy, and dreams start to feel unachievable. Jesus pointed out that we can't serve two masters without winding up hating the one and loving the other.

Moses persevered and remembered that God was the source of the mission. We don't need to have all the resources at the outset of our mission to accomplish what God is calling us to do; the resources will be given at the appointed time. Look at Moses! He set out from Egypt with a city-worth of people and headed into the wilderness.

(And there is always a wilderness; any God-sized dream has to pass through the testing grounds of the desert.) When Moses set out to lead the masses, he didn't wait until he had all the supplies. He didn't rent U-Haul trucks, or figure out how much food they would need for forty years—no, he stepped out.

Here is my philosophy of life: ready, fire, aim. (Saying that always makes my staff and wife cringe a little bit.) Too many people say: "ready, aim, fire." If you do that, given the speed of our world today, you may miss out. Moses set out, and what did God do? God provided the resources one day at a time. Notice that if the people became fearful and hoarded God's provision instead of releasing it, the manna rotted. They may have been in an arid desert, but God brought water from a rock. Here is what separates success from failure and those who do from those who don't: successful people have a way of renewing and sustaining the vision so that it is not consumed; it does not burn out or run out.

Moses focused in on one thing—he would obey God and lead the people to the Promised Land. Have you figured out your one thing? Are you prepared for the distractions and detractors? Will you persevere? Just remember, in moments of darkness never doubt what God has promised you in the light.

Go Deeper

1. When have you felt led by God?
2. When have you felt stuck in a rut?
3. What do you see yourself doing in a few years?
4. Why is it important to get going, as opposed to waiting for perfect clarity?
5. Think about Moses' story, from the time of the burning bush until he saw the Promised Land with his own eyes. How did God continually lead him, even when Moses and others couldn't see what God was doing?
6. How does God bring our gifts, talents, passions, and experiences together for his purposes?

7. How have you seen God use your gifts, talents, or passion for his purposes?

Build Your Life Mission Statement

I hope that by now you are close to having a clear life mission statement. If you are still struggling, check out these examples from members of Ginghamsburg Church:

My life mission is to connect with the younger generation so that they aren't afraid of religion and start to turn away from it, to help them find their way back.

My life mission statement is to seek and develop opportunities to teach, mentor, guide, and develop relationships with retirees and retirement-age members and attendees of Ginghamsburg Church.

My life mission is to organize life groups to serve people in need by providing one-day home improvement services.

My life mission is to help children through the pain of neglect, feeling unloved, and living through the struggles of sexual abuse.

My mission is to end slavery, especially in sex trafficking. I want to use the strengths of strategic planning to grow funding and awareness for Ohio's link in the worldwide trafficking network.

As you can see, some of these life missions may have nothing to do with these people's careers. Your life mission might connect to your career, but your day job might just be your day job. In the previous chapters, you've laid the foundation for your life mission statement. Go back and look at your answers to the previous chapters' questions:

Chapter 1. Name people and qualities you admire.
Chapter 2. Identify needs in your neighborhood, community, and world.
Chapter 3. Look back at your struggles and how they define you.
Chapter 4. List excuses that prevent you from living God's dream.
Chapter 5. Claim your gifts of head, hands, and heart.

Now that the foundation is in place, it's time to build your life mission statement. Remember:

- this is not your mission; it's your part of *God's* mission.
- it's not just for this year or even five years; it's for your whole life.
- the mission should be challenging and may even seem impossible; that means you're on the right track.
- you may need to draft several versions of the statement, now and later.
- once you have a long version, try writing a shorter version to use in sharing the statement with others.

Spend a few minutes now working on a draft of your mission statement. Then, make a final draft, and illustrate or express the statement in a video journal or other document. Review your life mission statement often, and make it part of your memory. Take the rough draft or a final copy of your life mission statement and share it. Tell people about it, and invite them to pray for you as you live into it.

LISTEN FOR GOD

God, I am so thankful that you never let us go, in our distractions, in our false priorities, in our failures. Lord, clear our vision and renew our focus. Give us the courage to persevere. Amen.

WHAT'S NEXT?

One of my favorite stories in the Bible is Peter walking on water in Matthew 14. Remember that the disciples had had a big day, witnessing Jesus feed five thousand people. Jesus had sent the disciples across the lake by boat. A storm came and shook the boat, frightening the disciples. Then they saw a man walking toward them on the water. First, they thought it was a ghost, because, you know, that's logical. When Jesus called to them, Peter said, "Lord, if it's you, order me to come to you on the water" (v. 28). Jesus did just that, and Peter stepped out onto the water. As long as he kept his gaze on Jesus, Peter was able to walk on the water. All the while the storm was blowing around them, so Peter got distracted and frightened by the waves. When he focused on his fears instead of Jesus, he began to sink. Jesus reached out and saved Peter.

Sometimes Peter gets a bad rap for being afraid, but he was the only one who got out of the boat. His sinking was in no way a failure. Of course he was afraid, but he stepped out anyway. He wanted to be a part of what Jesus was doing, and the only way to walk on that water was to leave the safety of the boat.

Imagine yourself as one of the disciples, watching Jesus walk on water toward your boat. He invites you to come out onto the water. Will you go? What are you afraid of?

As you pursue your God-sized mission, at some point you'll need to get out of your boat. God is calling you to step out, to come to him. You'll need to trust that when you keep your eyes on Jesus, you will do things you never thought possible. When you get scared or afraid, Jesus will not condemn you but instead will reach out and lift you up.

Remember what Jesus said: "All things are possible for the one who has faith" (Mark 9:23). Pursuing your God-dream means understanding that with the God of the universe on your side, anything is possible!

NOTES

Chapter 2. Who Is at the Top of Your Ladder?

1. Gary A. Haugen, *Just Courage: God's Great Expedition for the Restless Christian* (Downers Grove, Ill: InterVarsity, 2008), 109.